1 MONTH OF
FREE
READING

at

www.ForgottenBooks.com

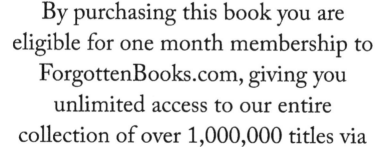

By purchasing this book you are eligible for one month membership to ForgottenBooks.com, giving you unlimited access to our entire collection of over 1,000,000 titles via our web site and mobile apps.

To claim your free month visit:

www.forgottenbooks.com/free1124708

ISBN 978-0-331-44342-4
PIBN 11124708

This book is a reproduction of an important historical work. Forgotten Books uses
state-of-the-art technology to digitally reconstruct the work, preserving the original format
whilst repairing imperfections present in the aged copy. In rare cases, an imperfection in
the original, such as a blemish or missing page, may be replicated in our edition. We do,
however, repair the vast majority of imperfections successfully; any imperfections that
remain are intentionally left to preserve the state of such historical works.

North Carolina College.

——o——

THIS INSTITUTION, under the fostering care of the EVANGELICAL LUTHERAN SYNOD OF NORTH CAROLINA, is located in the growing town of Mt. Pleasant, Cabarrus county, N. C., in the midst of a liberal and intelligent people, nine miles from Concord.

The Faculty is constituted as follows:

REV. LOUIS A. BIKLE, A. M.,
PRESIDENT,
AND. PROFESSOR OF MORAL AND INTELLECTUAL PHILOSOPHY.

REV. WM. E. HUBBERT, A. M.,
PROFESSOR OF ANCIENT LANGUAGES AND CLASSICAL LITERATURE.

H. T. J. LUDWICK, A. M.,
PROFESSOR OF MATHEMATICS, ASTRONOMY AND PHYSICS.

PAUL A. BARRIER, M. D.,
LECTURER ON CHEMISTRY, ANATOMY AND PHYSIOLOGY.

J. ADOLPHUS LINN,
JASON C. MOSER,
TUTORS.

Expenses per Session of 10 Months :

Collegiate Department, ...$147 00 to $167 00
Academic Department,.........................$132 00 to $147 00

———————

☞ The health and morality of the place are noteworthy, and contribute greatly to successful study.

The number of students in attendance last year was 131.

For further information apply to

REV. L. A. BIKLE, President.

MINUTES

OF THE

SEVENTIETH ANNUAL CONVENTION

OF THE

EVANGELICAL LUTHERAN

SYNOD AND MINISTERIUM

OF NORTH CAROLINA,

HELD IN

ST. PAUL'S EV. LUTHERAN CHURCH,

ROWAN COUNTY, N. C.,

From April 30th till May 5th, 1873.

MINUTES

OF THE

SEVENTIETH CONVENTION

OF THE

EVAN. LUTHERAN SYNOD OF N. CAROLINA.

————:o:————

In accordance with the resolution of adjournment, adopted at its last meeting, the Ev. LUTH. SYNOD OF NORTH CAROLINA, convened in St. Paul's Church, Rowan County, N. C., on Wednesday, April 30th, 1873, at 10 o'clock, A. M. The opening sermon, was delivered by the President, REV. W. H. CONE, from Acts xvi : 17.

AFTERNOON SESSION.

After a recess of one hour, Synod was opened by the President, according to our established order.

The roll was called, and the names of the members of Synod recorded.

MINISTERS.

1. REV. W. ARTZ,..Salisbury, N. C.
2. " S. ROTHROCK,...............................Gold Hill, "
3. " N. ALDRICH,..................................Charlotte, "
4. " D. M. HENKEL,*...........................Mt. Pleasant, "
5. " S. SCHERER,................................Gibsonville, "
6. " G. D. BERNHEIM,........................Wilmington, "

* Received at this meeting.

7. " W. H. CONE,.............................Gold Hill, N. C.
8. " C. H. BERNHEIM,........................Concord, "
9. " J. D. BOWLES,..........................Lexington, "
10. " Prof. L. A. BIKLE,....................Mt. Pleasant, "
11. " W. KIMBALL,...........................Salisbury, "
12. " A. D. L. MOSER,.......................Salisbury, "
13. " J. G. NEIFFER,........................Salisbury, "
14. " Prof. W. E. HUBBERT,†.................Mt. Pleasant, "
15. " J. H. FESPERMAN,‡.....................Statesville, "
16. " W. R. KETCHIE,........................Mt. Pleasant, "
17. " R. L. BROWN,..........................Salisbury, "
18. " E. P. PARKER,.........................Brick Church, "
19. " P. E. ZINK,‖..........................Lexington, "
20. " H. M. BROWN,‖.........................Salisbury, "

LAY DELEGATES.

Mr. MOSES A. BOST,...........From Rev. S. Rothrock's charge.
" A. ALDRICH,.............. " " N. Aldrich's "
Maj. L. G. HEILIG,......... " " D. M. Henkel's "
Mr. W. R. ROSS,............ " " S. Scherer's "
" JOHN MYER,............... " " G. D. Bernheim's "
" JACOB LYERLY,........... " " W. H. Cone's "
" ANDREW SINK,............ " " J. D. Bowles' "
" J. L. GRÆBER,........... " " Pr'f. L. A. Bikle's "
" CHAS. A. MILLER,........ " " W. Kimball's "
" J. F. MOOSE,............ " " J. G. Neiffer's "
" D. M. HARKEY,........... " " R. L. Brown's "
" J. A. HEATHCOCK,........ " " J. H. Fesperman's "
" MABANE INGLE,........... " " E. P. Parker's "
" J. J. STARRET,.......... " the Davie Mission.
" CALEB LEFLER,........... " Bethel Church, Stanley Co.
" W. T. H. PLASTER,....... " St. Enoch Pastorate.
" JOHN FINK,.............. " St. James' Ch. Concord, N. C.
" E. A. PROPST,........... " Union Charge.

Synod being organized, the retiring President read his annual report, which was accepted and laid on the table for further consideration.

PRESIDENT'S REPORT.

DEAR BRETHREN:—Another year of our ministerial life and labors, with its sorrows, trials and conflicts, is now numbered with the past, and we are once more assembled in Synodical Convention, under favorable circumstances; therefore our grateful thanks are due the Triune

---

† Appeared on third day. ‡ Appeared on fourth day. ‖ Ordained at present meeting.

God, for the mercies, favors and privileges, with which, He has so abundantly blessed us, during the past year.

We have met in the capacity of a deliberate, ecclesiastical Body, at the time and place appointed, for our annual Meeting. As such, it is our duty to consider the present condition and necessities of the Evangelical Lutheran Church, within the bounds of our Synod, and adopt such measures, as we are convinced, will most likely, increase her efficiency and her true interest. During the present meeting of Synod, we ought to show in our deliberations, that we are thoroughly imbued, in word and deed, with the spirit and mind which were in Christ.

As required by the Constitution of Synod, I now proceed to present a Report of my Official Acts, during the past year, together with such items, as may deserve your attention, during the present meeting of Synod.

OFFICIAL ACTS.

1. In September, in accordance with a resolution of the Ministerium, passed at its last meeting, I addressed a letter to the Rev. J. G. Neiffer, then President of the Eastern Conference, requesting him to inform the Officers of said Conference, that they were authorized to attend to the ordination of Mr. E. P. Parker, on the fifth Sunday in September, during the meeting of said Conference.

2. In the latter part of the same month, I complied with another recommendation of the Ministerium, by forwarding to Mr. P. E. Zink, a written permission to preach and labor until the present meeting of Synod, under the direction of Rev. J. D. Bowles.

3. April 8th, Rev. L. C. Groseclose wrote to the effect, that he had taken charge of churches in Union County, Illinois, in the bounds of the Synod of Southern Illinois; he also requested his dismission to that Synod. On April 17th, I complied with his request.

RESIGNATIONS AND CALLS ACCEPTED.

1. Dec. 2d, Rev. D. M. Henkel, of the Virginia Synod, informed me by letter, that he had received, and accepted a call from St. John's Pastorate, and entered upon the duties thereof, on the first Sunday in December.

2. January 14th, Rev. C. H. Bernheim wrote that he had resigned the Concord charge, as the state of his health would not permit him to continue in the active duties of the ministry.

3. Jan. 20th, Rev. A. D. L. Moser notified me that he had resigned the St. Enoch Pastorate.

4. March 28th, Rev. Prof. L. A. Bikle informed me verbally, that he had resigned the Ebenezer church, to take effect at the present meeting of Synod.

5. I learned through different channels, that the Rev. S. Scherer resigned the Union charge the latter part of last year, to take effect Jan. 1st, and accepted a call to the Alamance charge, whither he has moved,

but he failed to give me official notice in both cases, but on seeing me this morning he gave me a satisfactory apology.

6. Feb. 15th, Rev. A. D. L. Moser was requested by me to supply Union Church with preaching until the present meeting of Synod, with a view to a permanent arrangement at this meeting of Synod.

7. March 28th, H. M. Brown, a theological student, asked permission to supply Bethel and Christ's Churches with preaching until the present meeting of Synod. I gave him the desired permission.

INSTALLATION.

January 5th, Rev. D. M. Henkel was installed pastor of St. John's charge. Rev. W. H. Cone delivered the charge to the Pastor, and Rev. Prof. L. A. Bikle, the charge to the congregation.

CHURCH DEDICATION.

The members of the Church of the Holy Trinity were made glad, by the dedication of their new church in Mt. Pleasant, March 30th, during the meeting of the Western Conference at Mt. Pleasant. Rev. N. Aldrich preached the dedicatory sermon. Several of the brethren participated in the exercises, on the occasion. All the members of the Western Conference except two were present. The season of dedication was one of peculiar interest and encouragement to our people at Mt. Pleasant.

INSTITUTION OF THE CHURCH.

It will, no doubt, be gratifying to the members of this Synod, and the church at large, to hear that our Institutions of learning at Mt. Pleasant, are in a flourishing condition. We hope, that the legislation will be, with a view, to render them more efficient, and place them on a more secure basis.

VACANCIES.

The present vacancies within the bounds of this Synod, so far as I am advised are, Concord, Union, and St. Enoch Charges, the Davie Mission, Ebenezer and Bethel Churches. It will be the duty of this Synod, to make some provision for these churches.

UNION WITH THE TENNESSEE SYNOD.

I received a letter from the Rev. S. Henkel, Corresponding Secretary of the Tennessee Synod, October 4th, transmitting to me a true copy of the following resolutions, passed by that Synod, at its last Convention :

a. " *Resolved*, That we heartily endorse the sentiments of the North Carolina Synod, expressed in these resolutions, viz: that a union of the two Synods in a joint Synod, is both practicable, and desirable.

b. *Resolved*, That we entirely approve the action of the N. C. Synod in reference to this Union.

c. *Resolved*, That this Synod is ready to meet the N. C. Synod in a joint Convention, at any time and place, and on any basis of lay-representation, that may be agreed upon, by the Presidents of the Synods interested."

In addition to the above, Synod withdrew its suggestions of changes in the Basis of Union. The fraternal regard shown, in so doing, is very commendable, and augers well for such a harmonious Union as we desire. In view of the fact, that all difficulties have been removed, it remains for this Synod to take further steps, with regard to the Union.

And now may the Great Head of the Church preside over all our deliberations, that they may conduce to the enlargement, and sanctification of his kingdom.

W. H. CONE.

The annual election for officers now took place, which resulted as follows:

> REV. J. D. BOWLES, *President.*
> " A. D. L. MOSER, *Rec. Secretary.*
> " PROF. W. E. HUBBERT, *Cor. Secretary.*
> MAJ. L. G. HEILIG, *Treasurer.*

The Ministers then read their reports on the state of the Church, also, on their salaries and donations; and the Secretary read the reports from the Church Councils. These papers were placed in the hands of the President to be referred to the proper Committee.

Synod took a short recess, to allow the officers time to arrange the Committees. After which the President announced the following

STANDING COMMITTEES.

On President's Report.—Revs. S. Rothrock, W. Kimball, and Mr. Andrew Sink.

On state of the Church.—Revs. N. Aldrich, E. P. Parker, and Mr. W. T. H. Plaster.

On Church Institutions and Education.—Revs. G. D. Bernheim, J. G. Neiffer, and Mr. J. F. Moose.

On Missions.—Rev. C. H. Bernheim, R. L. Brown, and Mr. E. A. Propst.

On Unfinished Business.—Revs. W. R. Ketchie, W. Artz, and Mr. John Myer.

On Proceedings of Conferences.—Revs. S. Scherer, W. Kimball, and Mr. W. R. Ross.

On Petitions.—Revs. J. G. Neiffer, S. Scherer, and Mr. Moses Bost.

On Vacancies.—Revs. W. H. Cone, S. Rothrock, and Mr. Jacob Lyerly.

On Finance.—Rev. Prof. L. A. Bikle, Messrs. John Fink, and J. L. Græber.

Synod then adjourned, to meet again on to-morrow morning at 9 o'clock. Closed with prayer, by Rev. E. P. Parker.

————o————

SECOND DAY—Morning Session.

Thursday, May 1st, 1873.

Synod convened and was opened with singing, and prayer was offered by Rev. N. Aldrich.

The roll was called, and the minuets of yesterday read and confirmed.

REPORT. OF THE CORRESPONDING DELEGATE TO THE SOUTH CAROLINA SYNOD.

Your delegate attended the meeting of the South Carolina Synod, held in the second week in October 1872, and was cordially received by that body. The friendly relations so long existing between the two Synods is still maintained, and is sincerely hoped by both bodies to continue as long as the duration of time.

It is true that the brethren of the South Carolina Synod in general regret the withdrawal of our Synod from the Southern General Synod, but that action need not disturb the friendly relations existing for so many years between the two bodies; this is the feeling of the members of our sister Synod, and I assured them that such are, also, the sentiments of this Synod.

The South Carolina Synod is doing a great work in education and missions. Newberry College at Walhalla is prosperous under the able management of Dr. Smeltzer, and the Synod is making great efforts to relieve it from all pecuniary embarrassments.

In all their benevolent enterprises for the welfare and prosperity of the Church, we do heartily wish them God's speed.

Respectfully submitted,

G. D. BERNHEIM.

The above report was received and adopted.

Rev. A. J. Fox, M. D., now appeared as the Corresponding Delegate from the Tennessee Synod, and was cordially received and invited to a seat, and requested to participate in our deliberations.

REPORT ON MISSIONS.

Your Committee has nothing special to report. No papers have been placed in their hands.

We recommend that the plan adopted by this body at its last session to put into the bounds of our Church an active Missionary, with its connected regulations be continued.

Respectfully submitted,

C. H. BERNHEIM,
R. L. BROWN,
E. A. PROPST.

The above report was received and adopted.

REPORT ON THE STATE OF THE CHURCH.

Your Committee having considered the various reports of the Pastors and delegates, present the following as an embodiment of the whole,—

The condition of the various charges within the bounds of Synod, is evidence of the fidelity of our Pastors in the discharge of their duties. No complaints have come up from the Churches, but on the contrary, the testimony is, that the Church is in a healthful and growing condition. The word has been faithfully preached, the order of the Church service for the most part, observed; applicants for membership to the Church, duly instructed; and as a result of the whole, a rich harvest of precious souls have been reaped. The Lord has smiled upon the labors of servants, and gladdened their hearts with rich tokens of his favor.

There seems, also, to be, on the part of the members of our Church, a higher appreciation of the worth of the ministry, as manifested in the general promptitude with which they have paid the salaries of their pastors, the concern taken in their temporal welfare, and in some instances, in increased contributions to their support.

But in making this statement, we do not mean to declare that all has been done in this direction, that can be done. There is yet room for improvement, but still the marks of the present incline us to hope that the day is not distant when the Scriptural injunction, " They who preach the Gospel should live by the Gospel," will be fully recognized.

Respectfully submitted,

N. ALDRICH,
E. P. PARKER,
W. T. H. PLASTER.

The above report was received and adopted.

Parochial Reports were called for and handed to the Secretary.

B2

PAROCHIAL REPORTS.

MINISTERS REPORTING.	General	Local	Synodical	Missionary	Educational	Prayer Meetings	Bible Classes	Scholars	Teachers	Sunday Schools	Funerals	Death of Memb'rs	Expulsions	Dismissions	Restorations	Admissions	Confirmations	Communicants	Baptisms Infa't	Baptisms Adult	Congregations
Rev. S. ROTHROCK,	$15.00	$700.00	$10.85	$13.15	$6.00	0	1	50	6	1	9	3	1	0	0	0	7	120	10	0	2
" N. ALDRICH,	68.00					0	1			1	1	0	0	0	0	5	1	51	3	0	1
" D. M. HENKEL,		30.00	8.00	11.80		0	0	60	10	0	0	6	0	3	0	0	0	300	0	0	2
" S. SCHERER,	66.50	750.00	5.00	25.00		0	0	85	9	1	8	2	2	0	0	24	7	300	17	2	2
" G. D. BERNHEIM,		50.00				0	0	120	24	1	8	7	0	6	0	4	9	273	15	0	1
" W. H. CONE,	31.30	10.00	16.35	10.45	24.25	0	5	97	10	2	9	2	0	2	6	3	8	400	15	1	2
" J. D. BOWLES,	15.00		4.65	3.20		0	0	50	8	2	8	1	0	2	6	0	16	335	6	7	4
" Prof. L. A. BIKLE,		200.00	5.00	25.00	4.15	0	0	150	25	1	2	4	0	0	0	3	21	86	8	1	1
" W. KIMBALL,		310.00				1	0			2	10	0	3	2	0	0	16	400	16	4	2
" A. D. L. MOSER,	40.00	100.00				0	1	87	15	0	3	3	3	2	0	9	4	100	6	0	1
" J. G. NEIFFER,	7.30		3.15			0	1			1	12	4	0	0	0	8	4	112	10	0	3
" J. H. FESPERMAN,						1	1	110	12	0	3	1	2	6	1	1	2	180	8	2	1
" W. R. KETCHIE,	7.70	50.00				0	0	0	0	2	0	2	0	0	0	0	17	27	1	0	3
" R. L. BROWN,	6.50	3.90				0	0	0	0	1	8	3	0	0	1	3	3	390	13	5	3
" E. P. PARKER,	1.47					0	0	0	0	0	1	0	0	3	0	1	0	130	9	1	3
St. Matthew's church, Davie co.,	11.20					0	0	0	0	0	0	5	0	0	0	0	0	32		0	1
St. Enoch Pastorate,	8.20					0	0	0	0	0	0	0	0	3	0	3	0	250		0	2
Bethel and St's churches,						0	0	0	0	0	0	0	0	0	0	0	0	100		0	2
St. James church, Concord,	5.50					0	0	0	0	0	0	0	0	0	0	0	0	157		0	1
Bethel church, Stanley ounty,						0	0	0	0	0	0	0	0	0	0	0	0	100		0	1
Total,	313.47	2,203.90	48.00	53.60	30.40	2	9	699	69	49	82	43	8	74	74		1160	3784	137	23	36

Synod now took a recess till after divine service.

Rev. E. P. Parker preached at 11 o'clock, from Heb. xiii, 1.

AFTERNOON SESSION.

Synod was called to order by the President.

Rev. D. M. Henkel presented his certificate of dismission from the Virginia Synod, and was received as a member of this body.

CORRESPONDING SECRETARY'S REPORT.

I present the following report of my official acts as Cor. Sec. of the North Carolina Synod:

There has been very little devolving upon me. In accordance with the resolution of Synod, I transmitted to the Tennessee Synod, a copy of the resolutions relative to a Joint Union, passed at last session of Synod. I received a communication from the Cor. Sec. of the Tenn. Synod, relative to the subject, which I forwarded to the President of this Synod.

The following Synods sent us copies of their minutes:

General Council of the Ev. Luth. Church in America, sixth convention held at Akron, O., Nov. 7th—13th, 1872. Officers: Rev. C. P. Krauth, D. D., President; Rev. A. Spaeth, and S. Laird, Rec. Sect'ys; Revs. B. M. Schmucker, D. D., G. A. Wenzel, and Erl. Carlson, Cor. Sec'trys.

Nothing important was developed. But reports of the various missionary operations made to the Convention, prove it to be actively engaged in pushing forward the Master's work. About $45,000 were expended in the work, including the amounts of the District Synods. The true doctrine of the Church, at first confessed is still consistently maintained. Altogether the General Council has had a marked effect on the progress of the Lutheran Church in this Country, doing more itself, than all the Synods together previous to its organization.

Ministerium of Penn. Officers, Rev. C. W. Schaffer, D. D., President; Revs. F. Walz, and J. W. Hassler, Secretaries. Last Convention was held in Philadelphia. The Parochial Report shows, Ministers, 161; Congregations, 327; Confirmed Membership, 63.548. This Synod is closely identified with the General Council, being, in fact, the chief agent in its formation.

Ev. Luth. Tenn. Synod. President, Rev. Dr. A. J. Fox; Rec. Sec. Rev. L. A. Fox; Cor. Sec. Rev. S. Henkel. The action taken by this sister Synod in reference to the proposed union, has been officially communicated to you, and hence requires no further notice from me in this paper. The Synod is evidently prospering, as its increased liberality and educational efforts prove.

Luth. Synod of S. W. Va., thirty-first session. This Synod being a daughter of the N. C. Synod, claims our fraternal greeting. It appears to be doing a good work in the interest of the Church. Officers are : Rev. J. J. Scherer, Pres.; Rev. J. B. Greiner, Sec'y.

Respectfully submitted,

W. E. HUBBERT,
Corresponding Secretary of N. C. Synod.

The above report was read and accepted.

TREASURER'S REPORT.

L. G. Heilig, in acc't with the Evangelical Lutheran Synod of N. C.
Received of Synod by face of notes, &c.,..................$616 95

CR.

By amount paid A. Foil, as per order,....................			$240 00
" " " Prof. L. A. Bikle,.........................			13 30
" " " Secretary for printing Minutes,.............			70 00
" " on hand,..........			293 65

$616 95

Respectfully submitted,

L. G. HEILIG,
Treasurer.

The above report was read and referred to Committee on Finance.

DELEGATES TO SISTER SYNODS.

South Carolina Synod.—Rev. J. G. Neiffer, principal ; Rev. W. H. Cone, alternate.

Tennessee Synod.—Rev. D. M. Henkel, Principal ; Rev. S. Rothrock, alternate.

Pennsylvania Synod.—Rev. Prof. L. A. Bikle, principal ; Rev. G. D. Bernheim, alternate, in place of Rev. C. H. Bernheim, resigned.

CLASSIFICATION OF TRUSTEES, N. C. COLLEGE.

1871.

Revs. S. Rothrock, W. H. Cone, Messrs. Daniel Barrier, and Monroe Melchor.

1872.

Revs. C. H. Bernheim, J. G. Neiffer, Cpl. John Shimpoch, and Mr. Caleb T. Bernhardt.

1873.

Revs. D. M. Henkel, W. Kimball, Messrs. J. L. Græber, and Maj. L. G. Heilig.

Resolved, That a Committee be appoined to arrange the additional six members of the Board of Trustees, of N. C. College, in such a manner, that two be elected for three years, two for two years and two for one year. Adopted.

The Chair appointed Revs. G. D. Bernheim, W. H. Cone, and J. G. Neiffer, as said Committee.

This Committee retired for a few minutes, and then presented the following arrangement which was received and approved.

1871.

Rev. W. Artz, and Mr. A. Foil.

1872.

Rev. N. Aldrich, and Dr. P. A. Sifferd.

1873.

Rev. J. D. Bowles, and Col. P. N. Heilig.

Respectfully submitted,

G. D. BERNHEIM,
W. H. CONE,
J. G. NEIFFER.

CLASSIFICATION OF TRUSTEES OF MOUNT PLEASANT FEMALE SEMINARY.

FOR ONE YEAR.

Rev. Prof. L. A. Bikle, Rev. W. H. Cone, Dr. J. L. Henson, and Maj. L. G. Heilig.

FOR TWO YEARS.

Rev. C. H. Bernheim, Mr. E. D. Lentz, Mr. Daniel Barrier, and Mr. W. R. Kindley.

FOR THREE YEARS.

Rev. D. M. Henkel, Rev. J. G. Neiffer, Messrs. A. Foil and John Shimpoch.

Rev. W. R. Ketchie obtained leave of absence till 9 o'clock, to-morrow morning.

Synod now adjourned till to-morrow morning 9 o'clock. Closed with prayer by Rev. S. Rothrock.

THIRD DAY.—Morning Session.

Friday, May 2d, 1873.

Synod was called to order by the President, and opened with singing, and prayer by Rev. D. M. Henkel.

The roll was called, and minutes of the previous day were read and approved.

Rev. Prof. W. E. Hubbert now appeared and took his seat.

Synod consumed all the morning in considering miscellaneous business, but arrived at no definite conclusion.

The hour for divine worship having arrived, synod now adjourned, subject to the call of the President.

Rev. G. D. Bernheim preached at 11 o'clock, a very interesting sermon on the centenary of the Lutheran Church in North Carolina, based on Joshua i, 5.

AFTERNOON SESSION.

Synod came to order at the call of the President. Rev. P. A. Strobel, Agent of the American Bible Society for the State of North Carolina, being present, was, on motion, received as an advisory member.

Messrs. H. M. Brown and P. E. Zink, theological students, were invited to seats.

After resuming the consideration of the miscellaneous business of the morning session, and discussing it awhile, the following resolution was passed :

Resolved, That in view of the difference of opinion among the members of this Synod, in regard to forming a union with some other ecclesiastical body, the subject lie over without further agitation, to be decided at the meeting of this Synod in 1878.

REPORT ON PETITIONS.

Your Committee would submit the following :

1. Is a petition from Ebenezer Church praying Synod to continue the services of Rev. Prof. L. A. Bikle in their midst, "as a supply, if not otherwise." We recommend that this be referred to the Board of N. C. College, as Prof. Bikle is in their employment, and that they have exclusive control of the matter.

2. Is a letter of excuse from Rev. J. H. Fesperman : He pleads sickness in his family, as the cause of his absence from Synod. We recommend that he be excused.

3. Is a petition from St. Michael's Church, signed by quite a number of members, to use in their services, the "old edition of Lutheran

Hymns," instead of the Book of worship. We recommend this be not granted.

4. Is a petition from St. Enoch Church, asking to be connected in a Pastorate with the Lutheran Chapel. We recommend this to consideration of Synod.

5. Is a petition from Macedonia Church, Company Shops, applying for aid, to remunerate Rev. S. Scherer, and E. P. Parker for preaching at that Mission. We recommend this to the consideration of Synod.

6. Is a petition from Beth Eden Church, Newton, N. C., praying Synod to permit Rev. J. G. Neiffer to supply them with regular preaching, until they can secure a regular pastor. We recommend this to the consideration of Synod.

7. Is a petition from Bethel Church, Rowan Co., N. C., requesting Synod to sever their connection with Union Church. We recommend this be granted.

8. Is a petition from Union Church, that if the petition from Bethel Church should be granted, to attach some other church or churches to Union, so as to form a Pastorate able to support a minister. We recommend this to the Committee on vacancies.

9. Is a petition from Bethel Church, Stanley Co., N. C., praying Synod to supply them with preaching. We recommend their application to the consideration of Synod.

10. Is a petition from Nazareth Church to supply them with preaching. We recommend that this Church be supplied by Mr. P. E. Zink, as often as he may find it convenient so to do.

Respectfully submitted,

JAC. G. NEIFFER,
S. SCHERER,
M. A. BOST.

The above report was received, but before it was acted on, a Committee of three was appointed to re-arrange certain pastorates. Committee: Revs. C. H. Bernheim, W. H. Cone, and Mr. J. L. Græber.

The report was then considered and adopted by items.

Under item 1, the following resolution was adopted:

Resolved, That this Synod recommends to the Board of Trustees of North Carolina College, that the President, Prof. L. A. Bikle, be allowed to continue his connection with Ebenezer church, provided it does not interfere with his duties in the College.

Item 2d, adopted.

Under item 3d, the following resolution was adopted:

Resolved, 1. That it is the judgment of this Synod, that the vote of St. Michael's church, excluding the Book of Worship, was injudicious, and will be productive of the destruction of the peace and harmony of the church.

Resolved, 2, That we recommend the use of the Book of Worship, and also the old General Synod's Hymn Book ; but that they use exclusively, in their worship, such hymns, only, as are found in both Hymn Books.

Item 4th was referred to the Committee on re-arrangement of Pastorates.

Item 5th was referred to the Committee on Missions.

Items 6th, 7th, 8th and 9th, were referred to Committee on re-arrangement of Pastorates.

Item 10th, adopted.

Nazareth church was, on motion, referred to Committee on vacancies.

REPORT ON INSTITUTIONS AND EDUCATION.

Your Committee on Education, would beg leave to report as follows :
. North Carolina College is in a very prosperous condition under the able and efficient management of its Faculty, enjoying a higher degree of prosperity than at any previous period of its history. About 130 students have been enrolled on its catalogue during the present scholastic year, exceeding the number of last year by 28. Steps have been taken to increase the teaching force as the interests of that institution now demand.

We recommend that so much of our Synodical funds be appropriated to aid the College treasury, as will pay the tuition of all the beneficiaries of this Synod, subject however, to such Synodical instructions as have already been given.

Mount Pleasant Female Seminary is in full operation under the management of Mrs. Hubbert and Miss Ribble, assisted by Prof. Ludwick in teaching the higher branches of Mathematics, and Miss Henkel as teacher of Music.

The patronage of the Seminary has been encouraging, some fifty pupils have been in attendance.

This Institution deserves the patronage of the Church. Its Board have done all in their power, towards making it a first class Female Seminary, and it is the wish of this Synod, that it will soon be deservedly so regarded by all the members of our church and the public at large.

G. D. BERNHEIM, *Chairman,*
JAC. G. NEIFFER,
JOHN F. MOOSE.

The report was received, considered by items, and adopted as a whole.

Mr. E. A. Propst obtained leave of absence until 9 o'clock to-morrow morning.

Resolved, That the President of North Carolina College report annually to Synod the number of beneficiaries on the funds of Synod; their names, their diligence, industry, and progress in study, and the amounts of tuition due.—Adopted.

The following preamble and resolution were adopted.

WHEREAS, The practice of giving baptismal, and comfirmation certificates has fallen into disuse, and thereby the stability in, and attachment for, our beloved Lutheran Church is endangered; therefore,

Resolved, That we recommend each Pastor to perform no such ministerial act without giving to parents or sponsers a Certificate of baptism, or the party themselves if an adult; and a Certificate of confirmation to every person admitted to church membership.

On motion, the Treasurer was authorized to pay the committee on investigation to Newton, their expenses.

REPORT ON PRESIDENT'S REPORT.

The Committee to whom was referred the President's Report, present the following:

The first item claiming the attention of this body, is the subject of a union in the form of a Joint Synod, with the Tennessee Synod. As the Synod has by vote, decided the postponement of union with any other body for five years, your Committee have nothing further to recommend on the subject.

Your committee recommend that the Report be inserted in the Minutes. Respectfully submitted.

SAMUEL ROTHROCK,
W. KIMBALL,
ANDREW SINK.

The report was received, considered by items and adopted as a whole.

Synod now adjourned until to-morrow morning, 9 o'clock. Prayer by Rev. R. L. Brown.

FOURTH DAY.—Morning Session.

SATURDAY, May 3d, 1873.

Synod met in accordance with adjournment, and was opened with singing, and prayer was offered by Rev. S. Rothrock.

The roll was called, and the minutes of yesterday were read and comfirmed.

Rev. J. H. Fesperman now appeared and took his seat.

REPORT ON RE-ARRANGEMENT OF PASTORATES.

Your Committee on the re-arrangement of Pastorates would recommend,

1. That Salisbury and Newton churches constitute a Pastorate.

2. That Bethel, Christ's church, and Jerusalem constitute another Pastorate.

3. That Thyatira, St. Matthew's in Davie co., St. Paul's in Iredell co., and St. Michael's church constitute another Pastorate.

4. That St. Enoch and Trinity churches remain a Pastorate, as heretofore.

5. That Union and St. Paul's, Rowan co., churches constitute another Pastorate.

6. That Organ, St. Stephen's and Bethel, Stanley co., churches constitute another Pastorate.

7. That St. Peter's, Luther's, and St. Matthews, Rowan co., churches, constitute another Pastorate.

8. That Sandy Creek, Pilgrim, Bethany and Beck's churches constitute another Pastorate.

9. That Frieden's, St. Paul's, Alamance co., and Macedonia churches form another Pastorate.

We also recommend that the above arrangement of Pastorates leave each Pastorate untrammelled in the choice of their Pastor.

Respectfully submitted,

C. H. BERNHEIM,
W. H. CONE,
J. L. GRÆBER.

The report was received and adopted by items.

Items 1, 2, 3, and 4, adopted.

Pending the consideration of the remainder of the report, the Rev. P. A. Stroble was invited to address Synod, upon its re-assembling after divine service, upon the Bible Cause.

Synod now adjourned until after divine service.

In the interval Rev. N. Aldrich preached from I. Peter, ii, 24, and Rev. Prof. L. A. Bikle conducted the solemn and impressive service of confession and absolution.

AFTERNOON SESSION.

Synod came to order at the call of the President.

Rev. P. A. Strobel now addressed Synod at some length, in behalf of the American Bible Society ; whereupon the following preamble and resolution were adopted :

WHEREAS, The Synod of North Carolina has heard with much satisfaction, the statement of Rev. P. A. Strobel, Agent of the American Bible Society ; therefore,

Resolved, That we endorse the Rev. P. A. Strobel as Agent of the American Bible Society, and recommend him and his mission to the fraternal and favorable regard of our people.

The remaining items of report on re-arrangement of Pastorates, was taken up and disposed of as follows :

Under items 5, 6, and 7, the following resolutions were adopted :

Resolved, 1. That Union, St. Matthew's, Luther's, St. Peter's, St. Stephen's, Organ and Bethel churches, with Christiana and Gold Hill prospective fields, be left free to make their own arrangements, and that they call a convention of delegates with the Pastors now serving them, to form these churches, &c., into suitable Pastorates, subject to ratification at the next meeting of Synod.

Resolved, 2. That each church and prospective field send one delegate to said convention, to meet at St. Peter's church, Rowan co., on the 13th of May.*

Items 8 and 9 adopted.

REPORT ON VACANCIES.

Your Committee on vacancies would report the following :

1. The Concord charge has been vacant since July 1st. As the charge is making arrangements with encouraging success to secure a Pastor, we recommend that the people invite any minister whose labors can occasionally be obtained.

2. St. Enoch charge has been vacant since the 19th of January. We recommend this charge for the present, to the attention of Rev. W. Kimball, as a supply.

3. Nazareth church, in Forsythe co., is now vacant. We recommend

---

* The following arrangement of Pastorates was made at the convention at St. Peter's church on the 13th of May.
1. Union, St. Peters' and Gold Hill churches.
2. St. Matthew's, Luther's and Christiana churches.
3. Organ, St. Stephen's and Bethel churches.

this church to the favorable consideration of the Executive Committee on Missions.

Respectfully submitted,

W. H. CONE,
SAM'L ROTHROCK,
JACOB LYERLY.

The report was received, considered by items, and adopted as a whole.

REPORT ON UNFINISHED BUSINESS.

Your Committee beg leave to submit the following report :

1. On page 13, of last year's minutes, we find the following:

"*Resolved*, That a Committee be appointed to carry into effect the above missionary operations, as soon as practicable." Synod would be pleased to hear a report from this committee.

2. On page 15 and 16, we find a requirement to this effect : That beneficiary students be hereafter required to give their notes for tuition to the Treasurer of Synod.—What attention has been paid to this requirement ?

3. On page 20, we find that the committee appointed at the meeting of Synod in 1871, on the subject of Sunday School Literature, Order of service for sunday schools, and catechism for infant minds, was continued. Synod would be pleased to hear a report from this committee.

4. On page 21, we find a resolution requiring ministers to see to it that their respective church councils will always procure for communion purposes, wine made from the grape. Has this requirement been complied with ?

Respectfully submitted,

W. R. KETCHIE,
W. ARTZ,
JOHN MYER.

The above report was received and adopted by items.

Under item 1st, the Missionary Committee reported that the way had not been clear enough before them, to carry out the wish of Synod.

Item 2d, attend to.

Under item 3d, Committee was discharged.

To item 4th, the majority answered affirmatively.

REPORT ON FINANCE.

The Committee on Finance report, that they have examined the Treasurer's report, and found it correct. They also report the following contributions for synodical and benevolent purposes :

1. Rev. G. D. Bernheim's charge :
St. Paul's church, Wilmington, apportioned $60.00.
Contributed, ...$66 50

2. Rev. D. M. Henkel's charge :
St. John's and Holy Trinity churches, apportioned $75.00.
Contributed, by St. John's $43.
     "   " Ch. of the Holy Trinity, $25—...........68 00

3. Rev. S. Rothrock's charge :
Salem and St. Luke's churches apportioned, $30.
Contributed, by Salem, 20 ; St. Luke's $10. Total, ...30 00

4. Rev. N. Aldrich's charge :
St. Mark's church, Charlotte, apportioned $15.
Contributed, ...15 00

5. Rev. L. A. Bikle's charge :
Ebenezer church, apportioned $15.
Contributed, ...15 00

6. Rev. W. H. Cone's charge :
Organ and St. Peter's churches, apportioned $55.
Contributed by Organ $41.25 ; St. Peter's, $13. Total, ...54 25

7. Rev. J. D. Bowles' charge :
Sandy Creek, Lebanon, Pilgrim and Bethany churches,
apportioned $48. Contributed, by Sandy Creek, $15.60 ;
by Pilgrim, $12 ; and Jerusalem, $5.70. Total,...........33 30

8. Rev. S. Scherer's charge :
Frieden's and St. Paul's churches, apportioned $30.
Contributed, by Frieden's, $14.80 ; St. Paul's, $5. Total, 19.80

9. Rev. J. G. Neiffer's charge :
St. John's church, Salisbury, apportioned $30.*
Contributed, ...30 00

10. Rev. W. Kimball's charge :
Lutheran Chapel and St. Paul's churches, apportioned, $50.
Contributed, Luth. Chap. $14.45 ; St. Paul's, $12.35. Total, 26 80
                                               ——
                                        $358 65

---

*$25 from St. John's church, Salisbury, to be reserved by Synod for paying the expenses of a Travelling Missionary, when appointed.

Brought forward, ...•...... . ...$358 65

11. Rev. E. P. Parker's charge:
   Lau's, Richland, and Coble's churches, apportioned, $25.
   Contributed, by Lau's, $4.20.; Richland, $1.40;
   Coble's, $0.70. Total, ...6 30

12. Rev. R. L. Brown's charge:
   St. Matthew's, St. Stephen's, and Luther's ch's., apport'd $33.
   Contributed. by St. Matthew's, $3.40; St. Stephen's, $1.75;
   Luther's, $2.55. Total, ...:.7 70

13. Rev. J. H. Fesperman's charge:
   St. Michael's, St. Paul's, Beth Eden, and Thyatira churches,
   apportioned, $40.
   Contributed by St. Michael's, $6.40; St. Paul's, $0.90. Total, 7 30

14. Concord charge, (vacant):
   St. James' church, apportioned $40.
   Contributed, ...,.,........ ....5 50

15. St. Enoch church, (vacant):
   St. Enoch and Trinity churches, apportioned $30.
   Contributed by St. Enoch, $7.70; Trinity, $3.50. Total,..:.11 20

16. Union charge, (vacant):
   Union, Bethel, and Christ's churches, apportioned $55.
   Contributed by Union, $12; Bethel, $6.45; Christ's, $1.75—20 20

17. Contributed by Beth Eden church, (Newton,)............:... 5 00
18.   "   " Mt. Carmel, (Cabarrus co.)................ 3 15
19.   "   " St. Matthew's, (Davie co.) ..../.... 1 47

   Total amount, ...$426 19

                                Respectfully submitted,
                                         L. A. BIKLE, Ch'm'n.

Resolved, That Resolution No. 2, on page 21, of last year's minutes, be
rescinded.—Adopted.

REPORT ON CONFERENTIAL PROCEEDINGS.

Your Committee to report on the minutes of Conferences, offer the
following:

The Western Conference held two meetings during the half synodical
year just closed. The first convened at St. Paul's church, Rowan co.
Sept. 27th, 1872. The usual business of Conference was attended to, and
the Word regularly preached: the whole indicating commendable zeal
on the part of the brethren.

The second meeting was held at Mt. Pleasant, N. C., March 28th, 1873.
At this meeting besides attending to the usual order of Business, a mat-

ter pertaining to the Church at Newton, was called up. This has already been before Synod and disposed of.

Your Committee is much pleased to learn that the religious exercises were unusually interesting ; and that "The Church of the Holy Trinity," was solemnly dedicated to the Triune God.

The officers of the Conference are Rev. W. Kimball, *President ;* Rev. A. D. Moser, *Secretary.*

The Eastern Conference held two meetings during the half year. The first meeting was held at Frieden's church, Sept. 28th, 1872. At this meeting the ordinary business of Conference was regularly disposed of, and on Sunday, bro. E. P. Parker was ordained to the Gospel Ministry.

The second meeting of this Conference met at Sandy Creek church, March 28th, 1873. Aside from the regular business of Conference, we see nothing of especial interest claiming the notice of this body. This Conference will hold its next meeting at Union church, on Wednesday before the fourth Sunday in September next.

Respectfully submitted,

S. SCHERER,
WHITSON KIMBALL,
W. R. ROSS.

The report was received and adopted.

Revs. Wm. Artz, Prof. L. A. Bikle, N. Aldrich, and Messrs. A. Aldrich, E. A. Propst, J. A. Heathcock, W. R. Ross, John Fink, D. M. Harkey, Mabane Ingle, and Jacob Lyerly asked for, and obtained leave of absence from further attendance upon the sessions of this Synod.

Synod now adjourned until Monday morning, 9 o'clock. Prayer by Rev. W. R. Ketchie.

LORD'S DAY EXERCISES.

A large concourse of people assembled at St. Paul's church on this beautiful day.

At 11 o'clock, Rev. D. M. Henkel preached in the church from Romans i, 16, to a large and crowded congregation; and at the same hour, Rev. P. A. Strobel preached from a stand in the grove from John v, 40.

An intermission of one hour ensued, at the end of which, the congregation re-assembled in the church, and the President preached the ordination sermon from II Tim. ii, 15.

At the close of the sermon, the President proceeded to ordain Messrs. P. E, Zink and H. M. Brown, to the work of the holy ministry, being assisted by Revs. S. Rothrock and N. Aldrich.

At the close of the ordination service, the Lord's Supper was administered to the members of Synod, and a large number of the professed followers of Christ.

May these delightful services be abundantly blessed by the the Great Head of the Church to his glory, and the advancement of his Kingdom.

FIFTH DAY.—Morning Session.

Monday, May 5, 1873.

Synod met and was opened with prayer by Rev. S. Rothrock.

The roll was called, and the minutes of Saturday were read and approved.

The following resolution was offered and adopted :

Resolved, That every minister of this Synod be required to preach during the year in his congregation, or congregations, one sermon at least on the subject of benevolence and education.

REPORT ON MISSIONS, NO. 2.

Your Committee on Missions would present to this Synod their second report, and would recommend that, inasmuch as " Company Shops " has been added to the Alamance Pastorate, and Revs. S. Scherer and E. P. Parker do not desire any remuneration for their past services, rendered at that place, that the petition from " Company Shops " for aid be not granted.

C. H. BERNHEIM,
R. L. BROWN,
E. A. PROPST.

The above report was read and accepted.

The following resolutions were read, considered separately, and adopted :

Resolved, That we deem it right, necessary, and a duty, for this Synod to establish a Lutheran Theological Seminary, somewhere within its bounds; and that at this centenary anniversary of the introduction of Lutheranism in this State, we make the commencement, looking towards the final establishment of such an institution, as a memorial of gratitude to God, for having blessed our Church for the long period of 100 years in this State.

Resolved, That our efforts be directed now, only, to the raising of an endowment fund of $12,000, no part of the funds collected, or interest accruing, be used until the full amount of $12,000, be raised.

Resolved, That this Synod will receive any collections or donations, or legacy for this purpose, and will sacredly and conscientiously apply the trust committed to its care, according to the intent of the donors.

Resolved, That all our ministers are authorized to act as agents, to collect funds for this purpose.

Synod now took a recess, subject to the call of the President.

4D

AFTERNOON SESSION.

Synod was called to order by the President, and proceeded to business.

On motion, last year's apportionment of the churches for Synodical and Benevolent objects, was adopted, to wit:

1. Salem, $20; St. Luke's, $10; $30 00
2. St. Mark's, Charlotte,................................... 15 00
3. Union, $30; St. Peter's, $10; 40 00
4. Bethel, $20; Christ's, $5; Jerusalem, $2; 27 00
5. St. John's, $50; Holy Trinty, $25; 75 00
6. St. Paul's, Wilmington,............................... 60 00
7. Organ, $45; St. Stephen's, 10; Bethel, Stanley co., $10;... 65 00
8. Lutheran Chapel, $35; St. Paul's, $15; 50 00
9. St. Enoch, $20; Trinity, $10; 30 00
10. Ebenezer, ... 15 00
11. St. James, Concord, ... 40 00
12. Sandy Creek, $20; Pilgrim, $12; Becks, $10; Bethany, $6; 48 00
13. St. John's, Salisbury, $30; Newton, $5; 35 00
14. St. Michael's, $20; St. Paul's, $10; Thyatira, $5; St. Matthew's, $3; 38 00
15. St. Matthew's, $15; Luther's, $8; 23 00
16. Frieden's, $25; St. Paul's, $5; Macedonia, $5; 35 00
17. Lau's, $15; Richland, $5; Coble's, $5; 25 00
18. Forsythe Mission,................................... 5 00
19. Mt. Carmel, Cabarrus co.,............................. 3 00

Total, ...$659 00

Resolved, That last year's Committee to carry on Missionary operations be continued.—Adopted.

Committee : Revs. J. G. Neiffer, W. Kimball, and C. H. Bernheim.

Resolved, That the thanks of this Synod are hereby extended to the members of St. Paul's church, and the citizens of the vicinity, for their generous hospitality during our present meeting.—Adopted.

Resolved, That the Pastor of St. Paul's church be requested to read the above resolution at his next appointment.—Adopted.

Resolved, That one thousand copies of the Minutes be printed, and that the Secretary draw upon the Treasurer of Synod, for funds that may be needed to pay the printer.

Synod now resolved, by ballot, to hold its next meeting in St. Paul's church, Wilmington, N. C.

Resolved, That when this Synod adjourns, it stands adjourned to meet in St. Paul's church, Wilmington, N. C., on Wednesday before the first Sunday in May, 1874.

Resolved, That 'it be recommended to our congregations, to pay the travelling expenses of their Ministers and Lay-Delegates to and from Synod.—Adopted.

The minutes were read and confirmed.

Synod now adjourned to meet at the above specified time and place.

The President now closed the sessions of Synod according to our established form.

A. D. L. MOSER,
Secretary of Synod.

—————:o:—————

MINUTES OF THE MINISTERIUM.

——

' FIRST SESSION.

The Ministerium was called to order by the President, and opened with prayer by the Rev. P. A. Strobel.

On motion, a committee of three was appointed to examine all applicants for ordination. Committee: Revs. Prof. L. A. Bikle, W. E. Hubbert, and G. D. Bernheim.

Rev. D. M. Henkel requested and obtained leave of absence from the present session of the Ministerium.

Rev. J. G. Neiffer presented the report from Thomas Southerland—colored man of Salisbury—in reference to the performance of his duties.

Rev. S. Scherer presented a similar report from Sam'l Holt —colored man—of Guilford county.

After consultation was held, the President appointed Committees, consisting of Revs. W. Kimball and S. Rothrock, and Messrs. J. F. Moose, and P. N. Heilig, to examine Thomas Southerland of Salisbury ; and Revs. S. Scherer, E. P. Parker, and Messrs. W. R. Ross and Mabane Ingle, to examine Sam'l

Holt, of Guilford county, and confer upon them such ministerial powers, as they may deem expedient.

The Ministerium now adjourned. Prayer by Rev. W. R. Ketchie.

SECOND SESSION.

The Ministerium was called to order by the President, and Rev. Prof. W. E. Hubbert lead in prayer.

The roll was called, and the minutes of the first session read and approved.

Resolved, That Mr. H. M. Brown be examined by the Committee appointed for that purpose, and that said Committee report at the next session of this Ministerium.—Adopted.

The Ministerium then adjourned, subject to the call of the President. Prayer by Rev. S. Scherer.

THIRD SESSION.

The Ministerium was called to order by the President, and opened with prayer by the Rev. N. Aldrich.

The examining Committee reported that they had attended to the examination of Mr. H. M. Brown, and find him possessed of the requisite qualifications for ordination, whereupon the following resolution was adopted:

Resolved, That the President preach the ordination sermon, on Sunday, and that Messrs. P. E. Zink, and H. M. Brown be ordained to the work of the Gospel Ministry at the close of the sermon.

The Ministerium now adjourned, subject to the call of the President. Closed with prayer by Rev. E. P. Parker.

A. D. L. MOSER, Secretary.

Mt. Pleasant Seminary.

—o—

FOR YOUNG LADIES.

—o—

REV. W. E. HUBBERT, A. M.,)
MRS. H. V. HUBBERT, } PRINCIPALS.
MISS MARY RIBBLE,)

—:—

**The next Session of this Institution will commence
August 4th, 1873.**

THE Course of Instruction embraces the usual English branches, Ancient and Modern Languages, and Music.

The rates of Tuition are very moderate, and the entire expenses as follows:

Tuition, per term of five months, ...$7.50 to $20.00
Music, ... 20.00
Use of Piano,................................... 3.00

The Modern Languages are optional studies, in which an extra charge of $5.00 is made.

Good Board, including fuel and lights, is furnished in the Seminary building, at $11.00 per month.

The Seminary is located at Mt. Pleasant, in a pleasant and healthful section of North Carolina, entirely free from malarious diseases. Access is easy from Concord, only nine miles distant on the N. C. R. R.

Pupils received at any time. For further particulars or catalogue, address,

REV. W. E. HUBBERT,
Mt. Pleasant, Cabarrus co., N. C.

OFFICERS OF
NORTH CAROLINA SYNOD.

REV. J. D. BOWLES, President.
" A. D. L. MOSER, Recording Sec'y.
" PROF. W. E. HUBBERT, Cor. Sec'y.
MAJ. L. G. HEILIG, Treasurer.

———o———

STANDING RESOLUTIONS.

I. RESOLVED, That we recommend to the Church Councils the propriety of adopting the plan of collecting the Pastor's salary by assessment.

II. RESOLVED, That in accordance with our Church discipline, chap. 6, section 3, the Church Councils be instructed to require every member of the Church to contribute to the support of the Gospel, except such as in their judgment are too poor to do so.

III. RESOLVED, That no minister in our connection shall be allowed to take charge of vacant congregations until they shall have satisfactorily met their obligations with the former pastor.

IV. RESOLVED, That each charge shall have an annual settlement with its pastor, and that each pastor be required to present to Synod annually, a written statement of the amount promised for his support, and the amount received by subscriptions and donations from each Church.

V. RESOLVED, That the Church Councils be required to send to Synod by their Delegates, a written report, stating the manner in which their Pastor discharges his obligations to his charge.

VI. RESOLVED, That these reports from Church Councils be read in Synod by the Secretary.

The next Annual Convention of Synod will be held in St. Paul's Church, Wilmington, N. C., commencing on Wednesday before the first Sunday in May, 1874, at 10 o'clock, A. M.

9 780331 443424